RIDING PEGASUS BAREBACK

RIDING PEGASUS BAREBACK:
NOTES ON GREGORY CORSO

Gregory Stephenson

Felix Culpa Press

Published by Felix Culpa Press
Felix Road, Felixstowe, Suffolk
IP11 7JD

ISBN 978-87-974375-0-6

Grateful acknowledgement is made to the editors of *Beat Scene, Eclectica Magazine* and *The Rain Taxi Review of Books,* in which certain of the essays in this volume have previously appeared.

Grateful thanks also to Raymond Foye for his kind help & to The Estate of Gregory Corso, Sherri Langermann-Baird, Executor, for generous permission to print "In the Madness of my Cellar", "Creepy Flower Peddler" & "Buddha". Copyright for these poems is retained by The Estate of Gregory Corso.

Cover design & layout by
Birgit Stephenson

For Birgit
in deepest cahoots

Contents

THE RAINBOW IN THE SNAKE

"I did not know that evil is nothing but the diminishment of good to the point where nothing at all is left." Saint Augustine

Abandoned and left adrift, a lyric derelict afloat at the farther margins of Gregory Corso's oeuvre, *Way Out: A Poem in Discord* awaits reclamation.[1] A poem for voices or a verse drama, *Way Out* was written by Corso in San Francisco in 1956, and published in Kathmandu, Nepal in 1974, in a limited edition. Never subsequently reprinted or collected in a volume, the poem is largely unknown to readers today and represents something of an orphan among Corso's published work.

The long journey of Corso's poem from inspiration and transcription in mid-fifties foggy Frisco to publication nearly two decades later in distant Kathmandu is convoluted, its meanderings engendered by changing aspirations, estimations and circumstances, and by chance. The poem was begun by Corso with a sense of confidence and promise accompanied by misgivings. In a letter to Allen Ginsberg written in August of 1956, Corso relates that he has written a second canto to *Way Out* and is the process of writing a third. Yet, already at this stage of composition, he expresses reservations about the piece, even stating: "I do not believe in my *Way Out.*"[2] At the same time, Corso has sufficient regard for the poem to include it among those he submits to Lawrence Ferlinghetti to be considered for publication in a prospective collection of his poetry (the volume that was eventually to be appear in 1958 under the title of *Gasoline)* and to submit it to be printed in John Wieners' magazine, *Measure.* Subsequently, though, Corso writes to Wieners, declaring that *"Way Out* is nowhere, really,*"* and suggesting that the editor choose another, more recent poem of his in its stead. [3] (Corso's demurral notwithstanding, an excerpt from *Way Out* titled "Yaaaah" appeared in *Measure,* of which more later.) Nor does Corso object when Ferlinghetti proposes to omit *Way Out* from the forthcoming *Gasoline* volume, the poet even stating: "I'm happy that you won't use *Way Out ...*" [4]

Presumably, the manuscript of *Way Out* was returned by Ferlinghetti to Corso who was then living in Paris. But how did the poem (or at least a canto thereof) come to be published by Bardo Matrix, an obscure press in Kathmandu? In an interview with Cary Loren for *Blastitude* magazine, Ira Cohen, co-founder (with Angus MacLise) of the Bardo Matrix Press, relates that "the way I got the Corso manuscript was quite remarkable."[5] The manuscript of *Way Out* was, he says, passed to him in Kathmandu by the Jamaican painter, Allan Zion (1930 – 2001) who had driven from Paris to Nepal in a Volkwagen minibus, bringing with him – among his paintings and belongings – Corso's unpublished poem. According to Cohen, "Allan Zion handed me a manuscript of Gregory

Corso's *Way Out* which Gregory had left behind in the early 1950s." [6](Cohen obviously means the late 1950s.) Cohen goes on to say that the manuscript "came out to ten typeset pages," and was published in 1974 by the Bardo Matrix Press, as Number 1 in their Starstreams Poetry Series. (It is unclear whether Cohen and MacLise obtained Corso's consent to publish the poem.) And, as in Cohen's view *Way Out* was "more play than poem," to celebrate the advent of its publication, "we performed it for the first and only time, giving a World Premiere at the Yak & Yeti Crystal Ballroom on October 11, 1974." [7]

Way Out is a compressed, resonant, self-contained myth, a mind-movie, consisting almost entirely of dialogue. There are eighteen speaking parts, including a protagonist, an antagonist, incidental allies, observers, intruders and commentators, two prologues, six angels, a star, and personifications of Truth, Lie, Law and Discipline. (The poet, Arthur Rimbaud makes a non-appearance in the poem. That is, his arrival is much anticipated by certain of the characters in the poem, but – like Beckett's Godot – he fails to turn up for the appointment or invitation.) The setting and circumstances in which the poem takes place are dreamlike and indefinite. Events and dialogue occur in a liminal realm that is at once grounded in yet exists beyond the material world. It is a region or state of existence encompassing theatres, bars, alleys and known geographical locations (such as Capetown and Johannesburg) yet inhabited by entities such as a sentient star, angels, wraiths and embodiments of abstract concepts. It is a dream landscape, a dimension where death can occur yet a state of posthumous existence simultaneously obtains.

The poem depicts events occurring in the aftermath of the murder of Sweetface (alias Yaaaah) by Ratface. Although slain, Sweetface continues to be present as a spirit, conversing and interacting with other figures in the piece. His central significance in the composition is established in the opening lines of the poem by the lamentations uttered by angels upon his murder, and is confirmed by his delivering the poem's final, absolving, resolving words. As his name suggests, Sweetface is the epitome of benevolence. But what is the significance of his alternate name – Yaaaah – the name under which he also speaks in the poem? Is it a roar of anguish or a jeer of derision? Does the name suggest a shadow self, a secondary or alternative identity? Perhaps the name serves to indicate a hidden aspect of his nature – righteous anger – as expressed when he violently puts an end to the character Ballpoint Sam, a figure who is the very paragon of destructive malice, whose misdeeds include breathing "rotgut" into the rainbow lungs of colored snakes. Perhaps because Sweetface loves, Yaaaah must hate, hate that which is wicked and wrongful.

Ratface is, of course, antagonist to and polar opposite of Sweetface. He is described in the prologue as "assassinator of angels," and "Herod of us all." His is a Luciferian malevolence, intent upon the annihilation of all virtue and goodness. One-eyed, he can only see evil, devise evil. Yet there is within him a latent, potent, irrepressible dismay that he is no more than a "vacancy." In anguished flight from his inward void, Ratface seeks to extinguish himself both through attempting transcendent union with a star and by undertaking to unmake himself utterly through a reabsorption into his father. In both of these endeavours he fails, rejected both by the star and by his father. Thus thwarted and left confined in the vacuum of his illimitable enmity, he is compelled to confront the excruciating ignominy of being absolved and loved by Sweetface.

Even as there is a latent, eruptive contradiction at the deep core of Ratface, the poem implies that Sweetface, too, may – as suggested above – hold within him inconsistent elements. Apart from putting to death Ballpoint Sam, at one point Sweetface speculates whether he is himself Ratface: "Am I Ratface / did I meet Ratface when I met myself / Face to face." In this regard, at one point, Sweetface also proclaims himself a "Hegelian," declaring that "the quantum *must* be exceeded." This utterance would seem to invite the reader to see the oppositional relationship between Ratface and Sweetface as a phase in a dynamic development process evolving toward the Absolute. Or, taking our point of departure in Sweetface's remark that "surely an oriental mind will think otherwise," the tension and attraction between the two principal figures in the poem may be viewed in another way. Ratface and Sweetface may be seen to stand in relation to each other as opposite but interconnected forces, aspects of an indivisible whole, in the manner of a Taoist yin and yang symbol.

Death by rat-bite, death by rhinoceros, rancour and ill-will, griping, sniping, love, music, beauty, forgiveness, the rainbow in the snake and its would-be destroyer destroyed – the world depicted in *Way Out* is an x-ray of our human life in time and matter, its evils and miracles, its mysteries. The poem may also be read as a mythic vision of the archetypal forces deep within our unconscious, exerting energy and influence upon our conscious lives. On this point, it may be pertinent to note that the poem appears to have had its origins in the poet's own sense of inner division and conflict. Writing on August 23rd, 1956 to Allen Ginsberg, Corso comments: "I am not Sweetface Corso but RATFACE Corso." [8] The subtitle of *Way Out,* "A Poem in Discord," would seem to provide further support for a psychobiographical approach to the text. Viewed in this way, the poem may be compared to a personal "self-state dream," a dream dramatisation seeking to describe, name and resolve intrapsychic conflict, the clash of opposing and contradictory desires and impulses within the psyche.

A stray, uncollected fragment of an original longer version of *Way Out* was (as mentioned above) printed in John Wiener's magazine, *Measure,* in 1958. [9] Titled "Yaaaah," the poem is a monologue spoken by Sweetface's shadow self/alter-ego. The piece is of interest not least for providing details pertaining to the circumstances underlying the relationship between Sweetface and Ratface. In the poem, Yaaaah relates how a youthful Ratface "bundled with lace," became defiled, was persecuted (stoned by children, losing an eye) and was given shelter and succour by Sweetface. (Symbolic parallels perhaps to the poet's own traumatic childhood and delinquent adolescence.) Somehow, in return for the hospitality and sympathy he extends to the injured Ratface, Sweetface becomes diminished, impaired, his musical abilities undermined. It is as if – in the manner of a black hole sucking in what is around it – the dense darkness of Ratface draws into him the light of others who are in his proximity, obliterating it in the lightless sink at the center of his being. Wounded, half-blind, self-pitying, Ratface, for his part, elects to return insult for insult, evil for evil, becoming "an assassin ... child of Death." Henceforward, like a pair of binary planets, Ratface and Sweetface, are locked in mutual enmity.

Expressed in *Way Out* is Corso's preoccupation with primal, perennial questions of human existence: the origins and nature of goodness and of evil, and the terms and circumstances of their contest both in the world and within the individual spirit. It is a theme to be found throughout Corso's writing, from his earliest poems to his final, posthumous volume. The theme is also central to his novel,

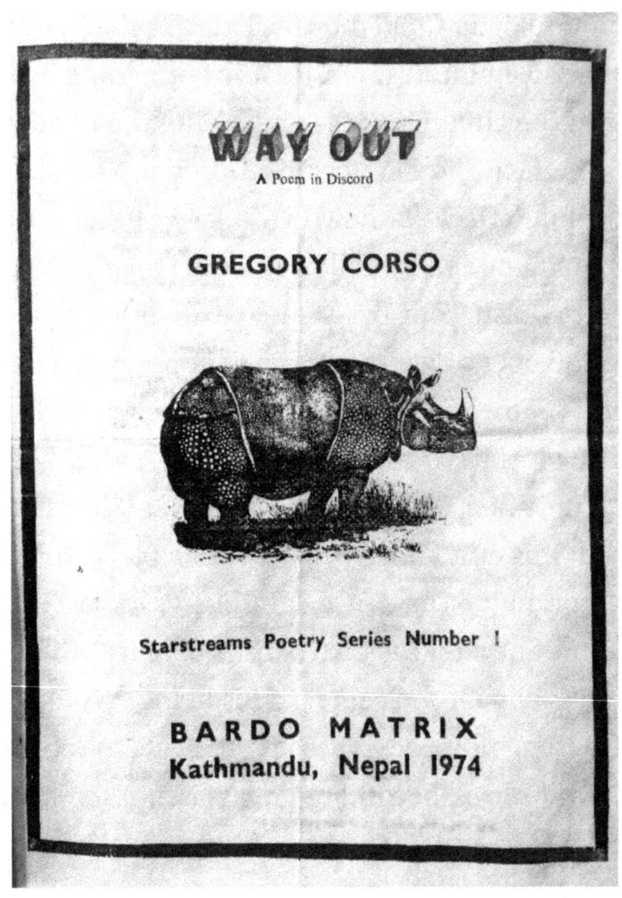

The American Express (1961) which depicts competing idealistic schemes and nihilistic conspiracies. [10]*Way Out* may thus be seen as a constituent in a larger mythopoeic pattern running through much of Corso's work. Flawed but vital, a work of raw vision, quickened with the poet's verbal energy and a surrealist whimsy, *Way Out* deserves to be retrieved and reprinted.

NOTES

---

[1] *Way Out: A Poem in Discord* by Gregory Corso. Kathmandu, Nepal: Bardo Matrix, 1974. Starstreams Poetry Series No. 1. Edition limited to 500 copies.

[2] *An Accidental Autobiography: The Selected Letters of Gregory Corso,* ed. by Bill Morgan. NY: New Directions, 2003, p. 8.

[3] *Ibid.* p. 64.

[4] *Ibid.* p. 49.

[5] *Blastitude,* No. 13, August 2002. Ira Cohen in conversation with Cary Loren. www.blastitude.com>ira_cohen

[6] "The Great Rice Paper Adventure, Kathmandu, 1972-1977" by Ira Cohen. www.poetspath.com/scholarship-project/cohen.htm (Originally published in *New Observations,* no. 106, May/June 1995.)

[7] *Ibid.*

[8] *An Accidental Autobiography.* Letter from Gregory Corso to Allen Ginsberg, 23 August 1956. p. 6.

[9] "Yaaaah" by Gregory Corso in *Measure,* no. 2, ed. by John Wieners. San Francisco: 1958, pp. 42-43.

[10] *The American Express* by Gregory Corso. Paris: Olympia Press, 1961.

Photo by Robert Wilson. Used by permission.

In a life of wide and restless travels, Gregory Corso produced six collections of poetry, together with a handful of plays and a novel, but left trailing in the wake of his urgent journeys an unknown number of lost poems. In interviews, Corso has recounted the sad loss of a suitcase full of his early poems in a Greyhound Bus terminal in Florida during the mid 1950s. [1] He has also lamented the theft of two suitcases of poems – four years work – left in the care of the poet Isabella Gardner at the Hotel Chelsea in the mid 1970s. [2] And he has regretted the sale to university libraries of his personal notebooks filled with unpublished poems: "When I needed money for dope, you see, I would never recopy the poems. I'd just sell the book. So a lot of my poems, you know, are in the universities and have never been published." [3] Other of Corso's poems would seem simply to have been scattered behind him, mislaid and left unremembered in the rush of further poetic inspiration and abrupt departures to somewhere else. I believe that this latter explanation is likely the case as regards the three poems that I have excavated, so to speak, from a recording of a public reading of his poems given by Gregory Corso at the Poetry Center at San Francisco State College in October of 1956. [4]

Corso begins the 36 minute reading with nine poems selected from his collection, *The Vestal Lady on Brattle* (1955), then reads eight poems from a manuscript notebook titled "Poems Written in San Francisco, 1956." Of these poems, four would later be gathered in *Gasoline* (1958), and one would be

printed in *The Happy Birthday of Death* (1960.) The three
fugitive poems embedded in the audio tape are "In the
Madness of my Cellar," "Creepy Flower Peddler," and
"Buddha." [5] Presented here below are my transcribed versions
of these three hitherto unpublished poems. I cannot, of course,
vouch either for punctuation, lineation or stanzaic patterns in
the poems as I have rendered them here. Moreover, in the
poem "Buddha," despite repeated listening to Corso's
recitation on the audio tape, I am not fully confident as to my
correct understanding of certain individual words. These
include "peril," "assayed," "infant," and "barium." (Alternative
suggestions concerning these words would be very welcome.)
And let me take the opportunity here to express my gratitude
to Raymond Foye for his gracious and invaluable help in
correcting my transcriptions of the poems.

IN THE MADNESS OF MY CELLAR

I lost my God in the madness of my cellar.
I watched the janitor scorch a sacramental rat,
beat it against the pipe, rub hot pepper in its eyes.

No loves, no loves, in the madness of my cellar.

My baby brother leans against the hot furnace.
My father hangs red peppers to dry.
And my mad, mad mother giggles to the tarantella.

CREEPY FLOWER PEDDLER

He sells flowers and is a creep.
He sells flowers and wonders why he cannot sleep.
Unlike most peddlers, he grows his own,
and cuts them before they're fully grown.
And here's his nowhere song:

Little flowers without a stem.
Little flowers without a stem.
Three for a nickel, who wants them?

BUDDHA

A Harmonic Motion
For Jack Kerouac, Buddha-Fish

Buddha is dead.
Dead in the empty lot, in the fish box.
Dead without peril or theory.
Dead rehabilitated to dumb heroism.
A dead Buddha cannot view the pint wine bottle.
What does Buddha know of pushcarts?
With Buddha died his children, speechless, enamored by
kind demons.

Sweet Buddha, where is he now?
Whose cowhorn is he sucking?
Buddha immortal mute suffering with mortal memories
has gone to the mountains below the mountains.

Strong solemn law inhabits Peril.
Peril is the demon.
He steals the angels of Buddha, puts salt on their wings,
handcuffs their brains to masculine limbs.
Who will talk to the demon?
Who will admire his new secondhand hearse?
Who will kiss his gnaw of eucharistic feet?
Lay their abundant blonde verse upon his gridiron?
Pluck wolfbane from his gargoyle-eyed, regnant skull?
Shoot a silver bullet into his dropping mouth?
Drive a maple stake into his reasonable heart?
Steal the soil of his native Transylvanian acreage?
Who will do this?
You will, children of Buddha.
You mad children of sodacaps.
You'll stick nails in the tires of his hearse.
Sip gasoline from the tank of his hearse.
Put rocks in the watertank of his hearse.

O Buddha, marled and gnawed, aimless in America,
in secondhand hearse parked on Pine Street,
watching children of love play, and on their knees pray
God the Father of ice cream.
O Buddha, ghouled and gargoyled,
bugged and assayed in the pale arms of Mother Death
Columbia.
Get thee beneath that pushcart and see it all.

See the broken glass and the bits of rope
that burst in on the radio wire.
Feel it, see it all Buddha!

Buddha is dead.
In death Buddha's skin is wet yet shaky
like penguin does ice water, the beads of life,
owing everything to flash light, nothing to sunlight.

I know you, Buddha.
When you were born, really born,
you was Brooklyn 33, New York,
a Jewish section where everything was secret,
like shopping bags.
Your home was a street with ground windows and wide
gray stoops,
with desiccant flowerpots and dry yellow curtains
 – all this would obscure your infant mother's twisted fate.

Bosatsu, now in motion.
Brother Bosatsu who teaches Buddha,
yet is engaged entirely in his own salvation.
Spit on Bosatsu!
Bosatsu who testifies the wisdom of Buddha and himself.
Spit on Bosatsu!
Bosatsu who strives to introduce and establish the ideal
land.
Botsatsu who dares set down into the realm of agony.
Spit on Bosatsu!

Now, Buddha, now that you're dead, what have you got to
say?

The back legs of a goat.
The empty matchbox.
The sweet spray smell of insecticide
or the old barium in a cow's hoof.
That's what I've got to say.

"In the Madness of my Cellar" depicts the traumatic encounter
of the poet-speaker with the cruelty and horror of the world,
an experience that serves to undermine his religious faith and
causes him to lament life in a realm without love.
Appropriately, the events of the poem take place in a cellar, a
hot, Hadean underworld, a realm of evil and pain. In addition
to the poet-speaker who narrates the grim incidents recounted
in the poem, the hellish cellar is inhabited by a sadistic janitor,
an apparently indifferent father, an innocent, neglected,
suffering "baby brother," and a mother driven to madness
(presumably by the cruel and loveless world to which, like the
narrator, she is also a horrified, helpless witness.) "Cellar" and
"tarantella" make an unusual and inventive rhymed pair
lending a subtle lyrical unity to this vivid, potent poem. "In the
Madness of my Cellar" resonates with motifs expressed in
several poems in *The Vestal Lady on Brattle* in which terror and
violence and innocent victims are prominent.

A similar theme informs "The Creepy Flower Peddler,"
where the peddler in question cuts short the lives of young
flowers, doing so for selfish commercial reasons. Already in the

title of this poem, Corso affects a reversal of reader expectations. Traditionally, the trope of the flower seller is associated with innocence, as Eliza in G.B. Shaw's *Pygmalion* and the figure of the blind flower girl in Charlie Chaplin's classic film, *City Lights.* [6] In Corso's poem, however, the flower peddler is seen as a man callously restricting the full development of natural life, and the poet views him as malevolent and despicable, another embodiment of the brutish and unfeeling life-thwarting forces of the world, another destroyer of innocence. On the audio tape of the Poetry Center reading, after having read "The Creepy Flower Seller," Corso remarks "I believe flowers should be left to grow, let them grow and let them die where they are, we have no right to take these things away from the earth." In this poem, the parallel constructions, repetitions, insistent metre and emphatic rhymes seem to suggest the narrow limits of the flower peddler's outlook.

In contrast to the taut structure of "The Creepy Flower Seller," the poem titled "Buddha" capitalizes on the deep resources offered by free verse in combination with epiphanic leaps of imagination. In this elegy – both brash and reverent – the poet contrasts the demonic, destructive forces of the world with those that resist such forces and whose aims are, instead, redemptive and liberating. Poverty, squalor, sterility and death clash in the poem with the teachings of "sweet Buddha," and are defied by the sly, joyous sabotage undertaken by the "children of Buddha," the "children of love." Buddha's insights are betrayed in this fallen world by hypocritical figures such as Brother Bosatsu (clearly undeserving of his misleading name) who seeks not the benefit and awakening of all sentient beings –as taught by Gautama Buddha – but only his own salvation. Yet, though "marled and gnawed ... ghouled and gargoyled," the spirit of Buddha somehow endures, reborn into the dessicated, spiritually claustrophobic contemporary world, and even in death remaining poetically eloquent, communicating through koan-like utterances.

Readers of Gregory Corso's *Gasoline* will recall that in the "Introduction" to that volume Allen Ginsberg quotes with approval a line from an unpublished poem by Corso: "mad children of soda caps." [7] At last, we know the source: the phrase occurs in "Buddha." Similarly, readers of Jack Kerouac's *Desolation Angels* may remember that in that novel the poet Raphael Urso (the author's pseudonym for Gregory Corso) recites to the narrator via telephone his latest poem which includes the line: "*Spit* on Bosatsu! *Spit* on Bosatsu!" [8] Again, the source is the same unpublished poem, "Buddha."

I think it probable that the three lost poems printed above – together with others written during the same period – were not discarded by Corso but were intended to appear in a collection to be titled *Early Poems* which was to be published in 1960 by the Totem Press. In a letter written from Paris in November of 1958 to Allen Ginsberg, Corso mentions that

LeRoi Jones (of Totem Press) wants to publish a book of his early poems and specifically names "Creepy Flower Peddler" as being among the poems to be gathered in that volume. [9] A collection titled *Early Poems* is listed as forthcoming from Totem Press in the bibliography for Gregory Corso included in *The New American Poetry 1945-1960* and is also mentioned in the bibliography for "Five Poets in their Skins," an article by Paul Carroll in *Big Table*. [10] For unknown reasons (most likely economic in nature) the book never appeared. We can only speculate as to what may have become of the manuscript of this intriguing collection. The recovery of the three lost poems from 1956 transcribed above serves to extend and deepen our understanding of Gregory Corso's work during the period between the publication of *The Vestal Lady on Brattle* in 1955 and *Gasoline* in 1958, and to remind us that further examples of Corso's rich, visionary, quirky early poems may yet be retrieved from manuscript notebooks and other sources.

NOTES

---

[1] "They were lost in a suit case at Hollywood, Florida … in the Greyhound Bus Terminal. And, Hope, my girlfriend – she went to all the Greyhound presidents to get the things back." Gregory Corso interviewed in 1974 by Robert King, "I'm Poor Simple Human Bones," in *The Whole Shot: Collected Interviews with Gregory Corso,* ed. by Rick Shober (2015) p. 108. See also letter from Gregory Corso "To Mr. and Mrs. Randall Jarrell" November 14, 1956, in *An Accidental Autobiography: The Selected Letters of Gregory Corso* (2002), p. 16.

[2] "So there was a big gap – 1970-1974 – four years work gone." Gregory Corso interviewed by Gavin Saleri in *The Riverside Interviews: Gregory Corso,* (1982) p. 32. See also "The Enigmatic Relationship of Poets Isabella Gardner and Gregory Corso" by Marian Janssen, *The Journal of Beat Studies,* Vol. 3, January 1, 2014, pp. 93-118.

[3] "When I needed money for dope …" Gregory Corso interviewed in 1974 by Robert King, *op.cit* p. 102.

[4] Magnetic tape audio recording of "Gregory Corso: October 21, 1956." Poetry Center Digital Archive. Diva.sfsu.edu/collections/poetrycenter

[5] From *The Vestal Lady on Brattle:* "Dementia in an African Apartment House," "Greenwich Village Suicide," "Coney Island," "In the Morgue," "Sea Chanty," "Vision Epizooic," "In the Early Morning," and "Requiem for Bird Parker, Musician." From *Gasoline:* "Mad Yak," "On my 26th Year" (aka "I am 25"), "Italian Extravaganza," "The Table was Hard Possible Music like Steel" (aka "This Was my Meal.) And from *The Happy Birthday of Death:* an early version of "Power."

[6] *City Lights,* film written and directed by and starring Charlie Chaplin, 1931. *Pygmalion,* play by George Bernard Shaw, 1913.

[7] "Introduction" by Allen Ginsberg in *Gasoline* by Gregory Corso (San Francisco: City Lights, 1958) p. 7.

---

⁸ *Desolation Angels* by Jack Kerouac (New York: Coward-McCann, 1965) p. 128.

⁹ *An Accidental Autobiography: The Selected Letters of Gregory Corso* edited by Bill Morgan (New York: New Directions, 2003) p. 184.

¹⁰ *The New American Poetry 1945-1960* edited by Donald M. Allen (New York: Grove Press, 1960) p. 447. "Five Poets in their Skins" by Paul Carroll, *Big Table* Vol. 1, No. 4, Spring 1960, p. 140.

COPYRIGHTS

CORSO BUT EVEN MORE SO

Fresh and brash, biting and buoyant, lyrical and whimsical, furnished with manic charm and quirky grace, Gregory Corso's plays can perhaps best be characterized as Corsoesque, that is to say altogether *sui generis.* Their nearest relations, I think, are the wild, iconoclastic plays of Alfred Jarry and Eugene Ionesco, but where Jarry and Ionesco are merrily nihilistic, Corso's irreverence is tempered with tenderness, and his anarchic humor ultimately an affirmation of truth and beauty. Despite certain stylistic affinities with the Theatre of the Absurd – bizarre situations, volatile characters, tragicomic incongruities, non sequiturs, radical juxtapositions, and a general disregard for theatrical conventions – Corso's plays have more in common with Attic Comedy and with the allegorical verse dramas of Percy Bysshe Shelley. These sources were, in any case, his earliest literary influences and inspirations. From them, he derived his exuberant satiric approach to the faults and foibles of contemporary society and his sense of deeper underlying metaphysical forces at work in the world. But, ever and always, first and last, Gregory Corso was entirely his own man, faithful to his muse and to his streetwise, off-center vision of history and human existence.

Gathering together for the first time Corso's far-scattered plays and adding to this heady mix two previously unpublished pieces, *Collected Plays* makes a lively, vital addition to the Corso canon. In a useful introduction to the collection, editor Rick Schober negotiates the sometimes perplexing evidence he has patiently mined from masses of Corso's manuscripts, notes and letters in order to establish contexts and a chronology for the composition of the plays. The first selection in the volume is a pearl, a prize, an almost-lost-and-forever-forgotten, end-rhymed verse drama written by Corso in the early 1950s, a play complete and entire but untitled and previously unpublished. Set in a posh country house in England, *Untitled Play* is a madcap comedy of manners. The civilized stability initially prevailing among hosts and guests in the house proceeds by degrees to collapse into delirium and disorder. Each of the characters in the play – beneath a courteous, cultivated exterior – is shown to be callous, selfish and cowardly, petty, pompous and hypocritical. Expressions of moral indignation and compassion among the participants are but casual whims, quickly supplanted by trivial distractions, backbiting and the satisfactions of self-righteousness.

By play's end, three poisoned corpses lie prone upon the drawing room floor. Though its effective fatal use is – in at least two instances – deliberate, the origins and original purpose of the poison in the play remain a mystery. Perhaps we are to understand that the poison is both literal and figurative, a representation of minds poisoned with selfishness and vindictiveness. Similarly, the persistent invasion of the

stately house by insects seems to suggest a kind of inward infestation afflicting the spirit, while at the same time it may be a harbinger of disaster, suggesting a judgement soon to be visited upon the house and those associated with it. In spite of poison and a plague of insects, to say nothing of the demise of three characters (and the unresolved mortal danger to another unseen, offstage character, a helpless child) the play remains light-hearted, blithely, briskly propelled by puns, jokes, preposterously extravagant conduct, comic incongruities and a succession of wildly improbable, unpredictable occurrences. Beneath the humour, though, serious questions are subtly implied: elemental issues of appearance and reality and of order and disorder. The contrast in the play between the pattern of rhyme in the dialogue and the manic behavior of the figures in the play is a deft touch.

The antithesis of the spiteful and malicious figures in *Untitled Play* is the eccentric, naïve, idealistic, unnamed young man who is the protagonist of *Standing on a Street Corner*. Set on the sidewalk of a busy urban intersection, the play is structured as a series of encounters between a young man with "little stars and angels" in his hair and various passersby. Open-hearted, enthusiastic and eager to be of help to others, the young man tries to assist pedestrians or to engage them in conversation, only to be rebuked or ignored by them or pronounced by them as being mad or suspect. The climactic encounter of the short play occurs when a sinister "tall man" takes it upon himself to disabuse the young man of his innocent views of the world. The play's ending is deliberately indeterminate. We are left uncertain as to whether idealism or cynicism will prevail in the world. An ominous sub-theme of atomic destruction extends and enlarges the central issue of *Standing on a Street Corner* and links the piece to *Untitled Play* with its suggestion of an imminent insect apocalypse.

Like *Untitled Play, Sarpedon* is a comic verse play cast in end-rhymed lines of dialogue. An additional similarity between the two plays is that of a shared theme of order versus disorder. Taking its point of departure in an incident in *The Iliad,* the setting of *Sarpedon* is the underworld, the realm of Hades, Lord of the Dead, upon whose much harassed, beset and beleaguered figure the plot action is centered. The central tension of the play derives from a dispute between Hades and Zeus over the shade of the slain Sarpedon. Again, as in *Untitled Play,* all of the characters (gods, mind you) are shown to be ignoble: self-pitying, self-seeking, resentful, covetous, deceitful and vindictive. Even the shades of the dead are prone to complaining, imperiously demanding of the Lord of the Underworld improvements in their eternal accommodations. At the outset of the play, all is in order, the divinely-appointed and time-honored system of the afterlife is functioning smoothly, running as it should, as per custom, but soon a disagreement arises from which ensues a sequence of missteps, relentlessly escalating in gravity. Hades' situation becomes increasingly untenable until at the last – such is the disarray now afflicting standard operating procedures in the underworld – the dead are in open revolt and hell literally freezes over. Disorder is again victorious.

A theme of order versus disorder likewise informs *In This Hung-Up Age*. The piece may be seen as a kind of modern Morality Play, in that the characters personify abstract qualities – altruism, gullibility, honesty, scepticism, impaired idealism, intemperance, practical authority, naivety, and beauty. The situation depicted in the play is also clearly symbolic: the breakdown of a passenger bus in a remote, desolate location, the ensuing breakdown of civility among the passengers, and the ultimate destruction of all (save beauty) in a buffalo stampede. (An interesting technical feature here is Corso's use of the figure of the Apache "a philosophical jazz enthusiast," as a parallel to the chorus in Greek drama, in that the Apache comments to the audience upon the characters and actions in the play.) In common with *Untitled Play*, *In This Hung-Up Age* is a critique of misguided social values and the dulled, diminished psychological state of contemporary humankind. The play contrasts the static, self-doomed era of pervasive materialism, debased taste, uncritical beliefs and rigid egotism in which we live with former ages when dreams were heeded, poets were celebrated, imaginative and creative impulses given rein, and beauty venerated. Like the bus, our mechanical civilization, Corso foresees, must ultimately break down and we will overthrown by the forces we have so long abused and ignored. Only beauty – the cultivation of which might have saved us – will endure the retribution soon to overtake our gimcrack culture.

Another previously unpublished poetic-dramatic artefact excavated by the editor from among Corso's archived manuscripts is a play in rhymed verse titled *JFK*. A note by Corso prefacing the play explains that the piece was "written in Greece 1960 after hearing the acceptance speech of John F. Kennedy following the nomination." Corso would seem to have drawn inspiration for his play from certain phrases in Kennedy's speech, particularly those in which the candidate pledges – if elected – to depart from the "safe mediocrity of the past" and to embark, instead, upon "uncharted areas of science and space." In *JFK*, the poet imagines the young president, having taken office, heroically attempting to change the direction of human destiny. In the spirit of Shelley's Prometheus, President Kennedy will set out, Corso envisions, to repudiate all the conventional, commonplace, perpetually vexatious and ultimately trivial issues of political ideology and international relations, and will, instead, redirect the resources and aspirations of the nation and the world toward the worthy goal of human liberation. This will be accomplished by an exodus of humankind from the bondage of time into the promised land of space, a journey from necessity to infinite possibility. In his pursuit of this noble metaphysical enterprise the president will be opposed not only by an obdurate old guard of purblind politicians but by the might and guile of Time itself. And by these conniving foes, Corso forecasts, the Promethean president will be defeated. He will, in the end, become engulfed by all the tiresome, paltry, metaphysically negligible issues that everlastingly distract humanity from its high destiny. The president's fate is reminiscent of that of the well-intentioned, idealistic young man in *Standing on a Street Corner* whose upright and kindly principles are undermined by the wiles of the sinister tall man.

The last of the plays collected in the volume, *That Little Black Door on the Left,* differs from its predecessors in that it contains no spoken lines. The action is performed entirely in pantomime – to the accompaniment of Berlioz' *Requiem.* The piece depicts the last meal and attempted execution of a corpulent (400 lbs.) condemned man. Once again, Corso attends closely to the descent from order to chaos, as the self-savoring ceremonious warden, the hypocritical prison chaplain and hard-bitten guards, and the avid executioner not only fail in seating their courteous, compliant but impossibly oversized prisoner into the electric chair, but inadvertently come to electrocute themselves. As if by an act of divine justice, the chaplain's Bible falls, striking a lever activating the electric chair, after which a sequence of errors leads to the demise of all the prison personnel. Still calm and dignified, the condemned man exits the death chamber, reading the Bible which he has retrieved from the floor. Significantly, in this play, disorder favours the disdained misfit, whereas in the text of the play the prison personnel are described in terms of animal similes. The executioner in his snarling frustration is likened to "a berserk seal," while the thwarted guards and livid warden are compared to "wild-eyed insane ducks." This silent darkly comic play evinces Corso's aim of continuing to explore in his work the potentialities of poetic drama, even proposing a wordless poetry, in which an unheard implicit poetry unfolds solely in visual representation.

Corso's plays are a series of surprise attacks on convention, necessity, self-importance, authority and boredom. Impish, impudent Gregory Corso, an impassioned poet-jester who (as someone said jesters occasionally do) sometimes "touched the hem of the metaphysical." Audacious, muse-driven Gregory Corso, bareback astride a galloping Pegasus. Our literature and our reading lives would be much the poorer without him. *Collected Plays* will be a blessing and a nectar for admirers of Corso's work, but would also make pleasurable reading for anyone inclined to enjoy playful – but pointed – poetic plays conceived by a rampageous imagination.

Collected Plays
by Gregory Corso
edited by Richard Schober
Arlington, MA: Tough Poets Press, 2021
130 pp. $14.99
ISBN 978-0578777016

PUTTING THE DOT OVER THE "i"

It was a combustive mix: an orphan, a grammar school dropout, an autodidact and an ex-con ravished by the English romantics, a street-surrealist steeped in the classics, an impish jester imbued with Greek, Egyptian and Mesopotamian mythologies, a rambustious poetic iconoclast with a penchant for archaicisms, a volatile compound of sensibility and swagger. Reflecting on the poetry of the late Gregory Corso (1930 – 2001) the phrase "internal combustion" comes to mind: compression, auto-ignition, energy. (Fittingly, his second and perhaps most famous collection of poems was titled *Gasoline.*) But there was always more to Corso's poetry than verbal energy and passionate vitality, it was also an art of oblique angles and displaced perspectives, of words set aslant and things eyed askance, of lyrical raids on the vertical world.

The Golden Dot: Last Poems, 1997-2000 gathers, as the subtitle suggests, the final writings of this hitherto so audacious poet. Through much of the time during which these poems were written, Corso was afflicted with the illness that was to be the cause of his death. Moreover, these same years saw the deaths of many of his friends, while the poet himself became reclusive. Reflecting this sere, severe latter era of Corso's formerly tumultuous life, there is a lessening in this collection of the verbal pyrotechnics and lexical somersaults that imparted such verve to the poet's earlier work. The poems gathered here are for the most part (there are notable exceptions) bare and spare, the tone conversational, the mood most often subdued. Even the punctuation of the poems is subdued: question marks far outnumber exclamation points, and individual lines, stanzas and poems commonly end in ellipses or dashes, suggesting the poet's awareness that there are few certainties in life, few topics which have been fully resolved, few matters on which a final determination can be made. Still, for any admirer of Corso there is much here to be relished. There is dash and dark fire, offbeat insights and a serious engagement with the unfathomable mystery at the heart of things.

Thematically, the poems fall into three groups: those engaged with the poet's personal history and present circumstances; those concentrated upon human history and the fate of humanity and the planet; and those concerned with cosmology, with the history of the universe, its origins and evolution.

"Redundant, chaotic, profoundly heart-felt, without order," so describes Corso these poems in a lyric titled "From birth to 80." (Nearly all of the poems in *The Golden Dot* were originally untitled, titles assigned to them by the editors for reader convenience are taken from the first lines of individual poems.) Corso's is an accurate, if incomplete, characterization of the poems assembled here. Among a number of other adjectives that I would add to the poet's own descriptive

42

choices are: candid and confiding, self-scrutinizing, self-assessing, self-recriminating, self-deflating, and unselfpitying. Corso's recurrent evocations of his personal history in these poems bear scant trace of nostalgia. Again and again, he returns to recollections of his lonely, loveless childhood, the bewildering brutality of his father, the aloof indifference of six sets of foster parents interested only in garnering the financial benefits gained by taking him into their homes, his repeated incarcerations in juvenile institutions and in prisons, the terrors and griefs, the wounds and confusions of a "lovelack boy" in a relentlessly unkind world. In a poem titled "I Can Predict with 99 Per Cent Accuracy," Corso encapsulates his childhood sense of isolation and vulnerability by deploying the metaphor of a foreign child riding alone on a train through nazi Germany, surrounded by suspicious, hostile faces. Yet revisiting in memory these painful long ago events impels him to attempt to understand the Great Depression-driven desperation of the impoverished foster parents who gave him such bleak accommodation and to attempt to be reconciled with the brutish father who mistreated and abandoned him.

Two luminous memories of his childhood cherished in poems here are those of his stamp collection and his discovery of poetry. In "Used to be Stamps of Egypt," Corso recalls the elevation and expansion he felt as a child in gazing on the colors and images of foreign postage stamps: the grandeur and mystery of the Sphinx on an Egyptian stamp, the heroic faces

of great men on French stamps, the paintings of Utamoro,
Hiroshige and Houkusai on Japanese stamps, the depiction of a
wild west cattle drive through snow on an American stamp,
kangaroos, musk oxen, gorillas. The little colored bits of paper
opened a world to him, proffering an exotic elsewhere in the
midst of the nowhere in which he was close confined. In a
dozen other poems, he celebrates the glorious occasion when
first he was visited by poetry. This crucial epiphany, occurring
while Corso was incarcerated in Clinton Prison, was preceded
by a portent – voices in his head whose words he recorded on
paper. Soon afterward, he discovered the book that opened his
soul: *Ideas and Forms in English and American Literature,*
Volume 1: Poetry, by Homer A. & James B. Munn Watt, 1925.
"Smart, Herrick, Hood, Marvell, Milton and the immortal
Romantics" induced in his young, damaged spirit transports of
joy. Poetry was for him both revelation and redemption,
offering freedom and agency, and – more fully, more lastingly
than his stamp collection – a shimmering sanctuary from
sordidness and banality . In a soiled, blighted world poetry was
a thing set apart, a thing exempt: "bright, flawless, eternal"
("Head Bowed Like a Bull.")

    There are wincing recollections of follies and failures of
later life: drunken antics, self-important facile
pronouncements, the time he callously abandoned a pet cat,
the time in Paris when a waiter knocked his teeth out, regrets
for his longstanding addiction to heroin, remorse for his

seeming inability fully to love another: "My lips took but never gave ... starved of love leaves one fat with emptiness" ("When Something of Power Dies.") Repeatedly, ruefully, he accuses himself of hubris, of having lived his life in a trance of ignorant pride: "Little did I know how little I knew" ("Not Recognizing Just the Kind of Person I Was.") Now, mortally stricken, contemplating his own imminent end, he gropes toward "Faith." He acknowledges that beneath the external, social personality, the defensive, self-protective face he turned to the world, he had long sensed "the emptiness gnawing at my spirit" ("In the End was the Word.") The form of belief Corso embraces is, of course, unorthodox, eclectic: "I hold the highest respect for the best of all religions / Impossible for me to embrace the entirety of one religion / I love like a box of wondrous toys the Greek gods of yore / And men of religion I honor are Jesus, Buddha" ("My Leadership Ability.") "Spirit," he affirms, is "Eternal and Absolute" ("Soul Sickness.")

A good proportion of the poems in this collection may be seen as fragments of an autobiography, the pattern of which is: self-discovery, self-betrayal, self-recovery. Poetry was, as noted above, Corso's salvation and an epiphany of vocation; his ragged, frantic life of drink and drugs is depicted by him here as both a violation of that vocation and a denial of what he truly was and of what he truly loved. Several of the poems record his current endeavors to recover what he feels has been forfeited and to redeem from a life of hubris new faith and humility. Humor also tempers Corso's confrontation with mortality. "I'm too old to die," he jests, and imagines making scary faces at infants in prams in resentment of their likely longevity or chopping down trees out of pique because they will outlive him. He envisions the moment of his demise: "I seep out airy & silent / singing celestial monotone," discovering solace in his posthumous condition as a de-materialized spirit, pleased that now he will be "more difficult to throw rocks at" ("The Need is There.")

Intermittently, bursts of cryptic lyricism erupt into poems concerning his memories and reflections – enigmatic passages unrelated to the immediate topic of the poem. These would seem to constitute testimony to the persistence of his earliest poetic impulse, the unconscious imaginative process that breaks forth in vowels and verbs, finding expression in lines that bear comparison with Corso's mysterious early image-rich poems, evoking worlds with words:

> On a tripod in the Gobi
> in a suitcase on the first street corner
> Who sold me? Who bought me?
> he with two hands on one arm;
> buy, sell, buy, sell, back and forth
> from hand to hand
> endlessly buying and selling me to himself –
> To rid myself of this insufferable redundancy
> I chopped off his buying hand ...
> ("Space Is In Motion")

at the moment before I acknowledge it
I arrive inbetween nothing ...
epitaphs sprouting from my eyes
nickels on my tongue ...
mystic with steel in sabbath dark
cockcrow in the courtyard blood
robed in high sentence ...
("The Muse")

There may be in Corso's mind and soul, at last, no definitive resolution to the psychological and spiritual issues with which he contends. In a poem titled "My Ancestral Home Was A Cave," the poet recounts a recurrent dream that may be construed as a metaphor for his life and for the current state of his mind and spirit. (The poem resonates with an earlier poem in the volume titled "I Am Frighteningly Lost.") In the dream he sees himself as belonging to a species of primitive man living during the ice-age, a man alone and cold, walking wearily, endlessly in a frozen landscape, through a desert of snow, lost, exhausted, starving, still resolute but just barely so, and deeply desirous of eternal rest and sleep:

I would be frost bitten
with puffed belly starved
trudging the wind snows
looking homeward in circles
encircled by mountains

no stepward path to climb
but ever upward
and deep within wishing
to fall where I can hardly stand
and sleep my life away –
("My Ancestral Home Was a Cave")

Natural history, human history and the ultimate fate of the world are very much in Corso's thoughts, as expressed in several poems in *The Golden Dot.* The extinction – sudden or gradual – of prehistoric species, such as the dinosaurs and the mammoths, the sabre-tooth tiger and the giant sloth, as well as of untold millions of molluscs, would seem, he believes, to portend the eventual doom of humankind, despite the confident affirmations of optimists: "Five layers beneath the mesa chunks of seashell / Hear the yea-sayers marking spots where dinosaurs fell" ("There were two times.") Other poems catalog the catastrophes of the past and the forces arrayed against our fragile race. In "Forces of nature," Corso inventories the multiple menaces that threaten humankind, including "Avalanches, tornadoes, hurricane, earthquakes, frenzied fire, squalls, el nino, cyclones – " and foresees "earth ill, moribund, dead ... Gone the whale ... Gone humankind, the lemur too – ." In "I wish I had a bear for friend," "The illness of winds," and "The 3 of Ice," he advances further evidence for the inevitability of some final annihilating cataclysm: contagion, an asteroid striking the earth, glaciations flattening the seas.

Corso is keenly aware of murderers past and present, tyrants and torturers, the Caligulas, the Hitlers, the evil deeds – great and small – of sick souls from ancient Rome to the streets of New York City. And yet, so astonishingly, so hearteningly, amid natural disasters and human lunacy, despite violence and greed, there have been, Corso asserts, great civilizations: Sumer, Egypt, Greece, Rome, Israel, the Orient, the Celts, Dorians, Eturians. And there have been great minds: Pythagoras, Socrates, Euripedes, Sophocles, Jesus, Buddha, Hadrian, Phidias, Dante, da Vinci, della Francesca, Shakespeare and a host of other poets, Hugo and Flaubert – paragons and heroic souls all. How to comprehend such radical inconsistencies within homo sapiens? Perhaps, the poet implies, they cannot be understood, only acknowledged, however sadly, as here in these poems. As Corso recognizes himself as a union of contradictory opposites, a "duad" (for so he names himself repeatedly in these poems) so too is humanity perpetually burdened with a dual nature, one that is riven with internal contradictions and inconsistencies. As within, so without, it is said, the macrocosm mirrors the microcosm. And, assorted perfectionist and utopian visions notwithstanding, no final resolution to the human predicament is likely to be discovered.

Beyond the riddle of human destiny are the mysteries of cosmology and metaphysics, still exerting a fascination upon Corso's imagination. Ever distrustful of doctrines and systems, he creates his own cosmic myth – "the Golden Dot" – expressed bit by bit through several poems in the volume. In Corso's mythopoetic cosmology, the vast universe – of which we inhabit only a miniscule portion – was generated from a primary singularity which the poet names "the Golden Dot." This mysterious, infinitely dense energy, this surpassingly compacted potentiality, exploded into the vacant space surrounding it, multiplying itself, combining into matter, generating forces and physical laws, ever expanding outward in all directions, assuming the forms of suns and worlds and all that exists. The poet foresees that ultimately the process will reverse itself, and the galaxies, the stars and planets and everything that has being will be drawn back into unity, merging, contracting, returning to the primal form of the Golden Dot: "The ever-expanding shall join the deflation of black matter / Black holes shall excrete Quasars / from the wide part of cone to the pin point of its end –" ("I know where the beauties lie.") When this contraction is accomplished, the poet believes, the process will then begin anew: the Golden Dot will again explode and expand, and "the beginning will begin again."

"Time passes in its arrival," Corso writes, "Space expands in its departure" ("Ask me not of moons.") The vision of such cyclic infinitude can induce in the mind a kind of vertigo, while at the same time offering solace, for while all is transient, yet nothing is lost. All that is impermanent and ephemeral returns to the imperishable, everything returns to the bright womb of being, there to be born anew. As in one of Corso's favorite Greek myths, the story of Demeter and Pluto, retold by the poet in "If I had strolled down the Via Sacra," in the universe at large there is a perennial alternation between life and death, between numberless muchness and next-to-nothingness, between infinitesimal finitude and vastest infinitude. The ultimate nature of the Golden Dot is an enigma and Corso seems inclined to respect it as such, to accept it according to his newly won faith. The universe, the poems here seem to suggest, is not a problem to be solved but a mystery to be revered.

The editors of *The Golden Dot,* Raymond Foye and George Scrivani are very much to be commended for their fine work in assembling Corso's jumbled manuscript poems into this worthy valedictory volume. Foye's introduction relating the harrowing history of the manuscript makes fascinating reading. Also to be praised and thanked is the Lithic Press of Fruita, Colorado for publishing this long-anticipated final work by Gregory Corso.

Like "time's wondrous play / on ruinous marble," ("Closing a file drawer") the abrasions of the years brought to Corso a rougher, huskier poetic voice, but one that spoke still with resonance and clarity, force and grace. *The Golden Dot* is a substantial, consequential collection. It will be of particular

interest to admirers of Corso's poetry, but deserves a wider
readership.

The Golden Dot
Last Poems 1997-2000
by Gregory Corso
edited by Raymond Foye & George Scrivani
Lithic Press: 2022
pp. 176. 20 USD
ISBN 978-1-946583666

GRAND LARCENY IN VERMONT: UNDISCLOSED EARLY MISADVENTURES OF GREGORY CORSO

Recently, I was surprised and intrigued to read in a post-humously published autobiographical poem by Gregory Corso, titled "I Was Born in 1930," the following lines: "I lived on the streets until 15 / I spent 6 months in Windsor Prison, VT / read *Les Miserables* there." [1] I was, of course, familiar with Corso's having been incarcerated in "The Tombs" (The Manhattan House of Detention) and in Clinton Prison, both of which experiences the poet has made reference to on many occasions, but this was the first allusion I had encountered to what seemed to have been an earlier prison sentence. For the poem goes on to state: "Spent three months free / and was sent back to prison / Clinton at Dannemora / Plattsburg, New York." [2] Corso in Vermont – the Green Mountain State – how unexpected and incongruous! What, I wondered, was young street-smart, consummately urban Corso doing in Vermont – so far from the Big Apple? And what had he done in Vermont to warrant a sentence of six months in prison?

My curiosity aroused, I contacted the archivist at the Vermont State Archives to ascertain whether inmate records for Windsor Prison were accessible. I received in return a reply from Ms. Mariessa Dobrick informing me that "Except for records pertaining to individuals who have been deceased for at least 50 years, records of individuals in the custody of the Department of Corrections are exempt from public inspection." Alas, a deadend. But Ms. Dobrick very kindly advised me that Vermont newspapers often reported on major and minor court cases and that these newspapers were available online. Following her advice, I subscribed to *newspapers.com* and searched the Vermont newspapers for the year 1947 seeking court or criminal reports concerning Nunzio Corso. (It will be remembered that Corso's official birth-name was Nunzio and that he later changed his name to Gregory, his confirmation name. Corso's sentence to Clinton Prison began in 1948, so if he had served six months at Windsor Prison and then three months later entered Clinton Prison, his sojourn in Vermont was likely to have been in 1947.) In the archives of *newspapers.com* I quickly found eighteen news items from ten local Vermont newspapers concerning the crimes, arrests and sentencing of Nunzio Corso, a youth of seventeen from New York. Indeed, sometimes the stories of Corso's criminal exploits appeared on the front page of these small-town newspapers; his misdeeds high drama, it would seem, in tranquil rural Vermont. In the following, drawing on these various news accounts, I will attempt to relate the sequence and nature of the events that transpired between July and September of 1947 in the life of the as-yet-embryonic young poet.

Vergennes, Vermont, State Industrial School

The first newspaper story concerning Corso appears in a journal called *The Bennington Evening Banner* on the 22nd of July 1947. The press report states that Nunzio Corso "who has been arrested twice in New York on burglary charges," was sentenced in a local municipal court on the 21st of July "to serve a term of two to three years at Vergennes on grand larceny charges." The charges of which he is reported to have been convicted are "having stolen money and clothing from a boarding house in Manchester." [3] Vergennes refers to the Vermont Industrial School, known also as the Weeks School, a reform school (that is, a penal institution for minors) located in Vergennes, Vermont. But what was Corso doing in Vermont? As to why he was in Manchester, Vermont, a clue occurs in a letter that Corso wrote to his publisher, James Laughlin, many years later, in mid July of 1961. Commenting on a reference to a ski-lift that Laughlin made in an earlier letter to him, Corso remarks: "great about your ski-lift, worked on one in Manchester, Vermont, when I was sixteen." [4] A further clue can be found in another article in *The Bennington Evening Banner,* appearing one month later, which describes Corso as having been "employed in Manchester." [5] Apparently, then, working on a ski-lift in some capacity was the nature of his employment and the reason for his presence in Manchester.

Only a month after this single mention of his crime and conviction for grand larceny in the *Bennington Evening Banner,* there is a sudden flurry of interest in Nunzio Corso in several other local Vermont newspapers, as on August 20, 1947, in the company of a fellow-inmate named Melvin Hill, he escapes from the Vergennes Industrial School. A search for the fugitives by local police is initiated and on the morning of the 21st of August, according to *The White River Valley Herald,* they are spotted "on the outskirts of the city" (presumably Vergennes) but they elude capture "by disappearing into the woods near the highway." [6] The same account goes on to mention that in the wake of the two boys' escape a dozen automobiles in the area have apparently been tampered with and that two break-ins have occurred. Soon hereafter, *The Battleboro Reformer* reports that on the 22nd of August, "Mr. and Mrs. Wayne Hill of Starksboro and members of their family woke from a sound sleep to find that thieves had ransacked the house, helping themselves to liberal supplies of food and items of clothing." [7] The intruders, we are told, "left behind them a pair of pants and a pair of shoes which authorities have identified as belonging to boys who recently escaped from the Weeks School." [8]

Corso's bid for freedom was short-lived. At 3 a.m. on the morning of August 23rd, according to a report in *The Barre Daily Times,* the Vermont state police placed him under arrest, "after a number of Hinesburg residents had apprehended the youth about two hours earlier." [9] In his possession were found "a 63 dollar watch and clothing, allegedly stolen from two homes." [10] *The Burlington Daily News* for 23 August states that Corso was "apprehended after he was found in the living room of a Hinesburg family." [11] The young fugitive reportedly told the arresting officer that he had hidden out in the woods near Hinesburg all of the previous day. Indictments against Corso were now to include, the article states, a new charge of grand larceny together with a charge of escaping from Weeks School. (Apropos of the 63 dollar watch, it will, perhaps, be remembered that watches for the young Corso held a particular fascination, as the poet himself has described in an autobiographical article titled *The Times of the Watches.* [12])

Initially, justice was swift and relatively lenient. As reported in *The Burlington Free Press,* on the 25th of August, in municipal court, Corso pleaded guilty to a single charge of grand larceny and was sentenced to serve "the remainder of his minority" (that is, until his 21st birthday) at the Weeks Industrial School, from which he had, of course, only recently escaped. In imposing the sentence, Judge John J. Deschenes told the youthful offender: "I am giving you a break by returning you to Weeks School. The law gives me the power to send you to Windsor (i.e. Windsor Prison) for this crime. By behaving yourself and co-operating with Weeks School Authorities, you may be released before you reach 21 years of age." [13]

State Prison, Windsor, Vermont

Weighty as they now were, Corso's woes were, however, far from being over. As ordered by Judge Deschenes, he was returned for confinement at the Weeks Industrial School at

Vergennes. A bad break for the forsaken seventeen-year-old, to be sure. But, Judge Deschennes had pronounced sentence on Corso for one count of grand larceny (the housebreaking in Hinesburg during which he had been caught by the residents of the home he had unlawfully entered) and there was as yet a separate charge pending for an earlier criminal act, also committed during the course of his flight from the Industrial School. This charge, for an offence committed in a separate jurisdiction and still awaiting trial, was for the forcible entry and burglary (on 21 August 1947) of the house of Mr. and Mrs. Wayne Hill of Starksboro, in which food and items of clothing had been stolen.

"Weeks School Escapee to Serve Prison Term" was the headline of the news story on *The Vermont Journal* for 11 September 1947, echoed in news stories in the pages of *The White River Valley Herald, The Bennington Evening Banner, The Barre Daily Times,* and *The Burlington Daily News.* The newspapers reported that Nunzio Corso, 17 years of age, of Brooklyn, N.Y. had been brought up before Judge Samuel Fishman in municipal court in Middlebury to face a charge of breaking and entering "the home of Wayne Hill in Starksboro on August 21." Found guilty by the court, he had been "given a sentence of from four to six months in the state prison here" (i.e. Windsor Prison.) [14] On the basis of Corso's reference in the poem cited above, it would appear that he served the full six months of his sentence in Vermont State Prison, Windsor, Vermont.

It's curious that Corso seems never to have mentioned these sad episodes of his early life, neither in the interviews he gave nor in the candid autobiographical essays he wrote. I suspect that his motive for this omission was not shame, but rather to lend a more dramatic coherence to his transformative experience at Clinton prison. [15] Corso did, however, in one instance, make imaginative use of his misadventures in Vermont. A poem titled "The Last Warmth of Arnold," appearing in *Gasoline* (1958) includes the following lines: "Arnold warm with God / hides beneath the porch / remembering the time of escape, imprisoned in Vermont, shovelling snow." In the light of Corso's ordeals in Vermont, these lines – though no less evocative and resonant in the context of the poem – seem now to be more poignant, more potent and more compelling.

NOTES

[1] *The Golden Dot: Last Poems 1997-2000* by Gregory Corso, ed. by Raymond Foye & George Scrivani, The Lithic Press, 2022, p. 30.
[2] Ibid.
[3] *The Bennington Evening Banner*, 22 July 1947, p.1.
[4] *An Accidental Autobiography: the Selected Letters of Gregory Corso*, ed. by Bill Morgan, New Directions, 2003, p. 287.
[5] *The Bennington Evening Banner*, 25 August 1947, p. 1.
[6] *The White River Valley Herald*, 28 August 1947, p. 4.
[7] *The Battleboro Reformer*, 23 August 1947, p. 4.
[8] Ibid.
[9] *The Bennington Evening Banner*, 22 July 1947, p.1.
[10] Ibid.
[11] *The Burlington Daily News,* 23 August 1947, p. 1.
[12] "The Times of the Watches" by Gregory Corso, *Cavalier,* December 1964, pp. 37-38 +.
[13] *The Burlington Free Press*, 25 August 1947, p. 2.
[14] *Vermont Journal,* 11 September 1947, p. 4. Also *The White River Valley Herald,* 11 September 1947, p. 4; *The Bennington Evening Banner,* 4 September 1947, p. 5; *The Barre Daily Times,* 5 September 1947, p. 7; and *The Burlington Daily News,* 5 September 1947, p.1.
[15] See "Poetic License: The Crime & Hard Time of Gregory Corso" by Gregory Stephenson, *Empty Mirror,* January 2019 (online) reprinted in *The Ragged Promised Land,* Ober-Limbo, 2020.